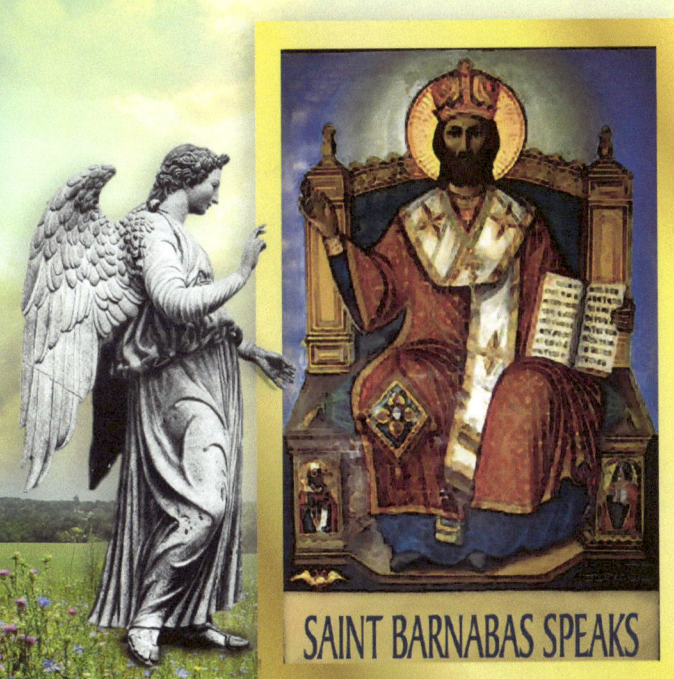

SAINT BARNABAS SPEAKS

MARIE-JOSÉE THIBAULT

Saint Barnabas Speaks - Book 1
Published by Abba Books LLC
abbabooksllc@gmail.com
Copyright © 2023 Marie-Josée Thibault

All Rights Reserved

No part of this publication may be reproduced, distributed, or transmitted in any form or by any means, including photocopying, recording, or other electronic or mechanical methods, without the prior written permission of the publisher.

First Edition, 2023
Designed and Edited by Abba Books LLC
ISBN: 979-8-9887805-9-5

Abba Books LLC
34972 Newark Blvd, #441
Newark, CA 94560

www.abbamyfatheriloveyou.com
https://www.facebook.com/AbbaILoveYouBooks/

S BARNABAS

Thy Peace on Earth must be achieved. No light, no litany must be spared to honor Thy Grace.
-Saint Paul

Preface _____ VI	Chap 17 _____ 39	Chap 33 _____ 77
Chap 1 _____ 1	Chap 18 _____ 41	Chap 34 _____ 79
Chap 2 _____ 3	Chap 19 _____ 43	Chap 35 _____ 81
Chap 3 _____ 5	Chap 20 _____ 45	Chap 36 _____ 85
Chap 4 _____ 7	Chap 21 _____ 49	Chap 37 _____ 87
Chap 5 _____ 9	Chap 22 _____ 51	Chap 38 _____ 89
Chap 6 _____ 13	Chap 23 _____ 53	Chap 39 _____ 91
Chap 7 _____ 15	Chap 24 _____ 55	Chap 40 _____ 93
Chap 8 _____ 17	Chap 25 _____ 57	Chap 41 _____ 97
Chap 9 _____ 19	Chap 26 _____ 61	Chap 42 _____ 99
Chap 10 _____ 21	Chap 27 _____ 63	Chap 43 _____ 101
Chap 11 _____ 25	Chap 28 _____ 65	Chap 44 _____ 103
Chap 12 _____ 27	Chap 29 _____ 67	Chap 45 _____ 105
Chap 13 _____ 29	Chap 30 _____ 69	Chap 46 _____ 107
Chap 14 _____ 31	Chap 31 _____ 73	Chap 47 _____ 109
Chap 15 _____ 33	Chap 32 _____ 75	Chap 48 _____ 111
Chap 16 _____ 36		

Preface

Embark on a wonderful journey with Barnabas and explore the mysteries of the kingdoms of creation! Barnabas is a handsome, blond-haired saint who wears a pristine white tunic and a contagious smile. Barnabas visits me often, and we pray together with joy and serenity.

Barnabas collaborates intimately with Saint Paul the Apostle in Heaven, as they worked together on earth as missionaries. He has explained to me how, through the Holy Spirit, saints in heaven are allowed to visit us whenever they wish—no matter where we are going, what we are thinking about, or what we are doing.

His revelations are quite unique, as Barnabas is a protector and lover of the environment! His book teaches us about the secrets of life hidden in the kingdoms of creation. He explains the importance of harmonizing oneself to all forms of life: fellow humans as well as members of the animal, plant, and mineral kingdoms that come one's way. Many mysteries are revealed in this book, including the unique spirits of plants (called elementals) and their incredible purpose, which was designed by God.

Join me and Barnabas and walk the path towards deepening your understanding of nature!

Barnabas, I love you!

Marie-Josée

Saint Barnabas Speaks

My children of a slumbering earth, wake up! I am pleased to speak to you today through the essence of Saint Paul on earth, my Friend in the Good News.

Verily, verily I say unto you, your mind is asleep: wake up! Look around you; see the misdeeds of the passage of men on earth! Acknowledge your determination to destroy this planet, entirely created by God, and ask Him for His Mercy! For each instance on your behalf, which resulted in a breach in the harmony of the natural ecology on earth, will be held accountable before God.

This is serious: rendering accounts before God is coming shortly. Let us be thankful to God for allowing you to read my Divine and Sacred words today. Amen. Alleluia!

Saint Barnabas Speaks

My children, rejoice and be glad, for God the Father Almighty is Merciful unto you today.

By virtue of the merits earned by the five crosses, which began in the days when I, Saint Barnabas, and my Friend Saul who became Paul and then Saint Paul, travelled through several countries in order to spread the Good News of the Kingdom of God, I have been allowed to speak to you in my own Voice.

For Saint Paul and I are forming a Teaching Team in Heaven, here in Paradise where we dwell, as we did before on earth; and now we are continuing our mission through the essence of Saint Paul on earth, Marie-Josée T., the one taking this dictation on my part today.

Many revelations are offered in this book, and I thank from the bottom of my heart God the Father Almighty, as well as Christ Jesus, our Savior to all, the Virgin Mary, Mother to all, and Saint Paul, our Friend to all.

Alleluia! Alleluia! Alleluia! Blessed be Marie-Josée who is performing her mission on earth to perfection. Amen! Alleluia!

Saint Barnabas Speaks

My children, remain in the hope of the Kingdom of God. When I traveled in Asia Minor with my Friend Paul, we were messengers of God and of His Kingdom.

Now, through our efforts on earth as in Heaven, we are continuing our mission in the same way: with faith and conviction, with zeal and fervor, and with the help of Christ, our Savior and our God. For Jesus Christ Himself is at the heart of everything we do, as He was 2,000 years ago.

Alleluia! Alleluia! Alleluia! Blessed is he who has faith in Christ Jesus our Savior, for this one will be saved and will be sheltered in the Kingdom of His Father. Amen. Alleluia!

Saint Barnabas Speaks

My children of the earth in great danger, I hasten to speak to you today about my life on earth.

I met Paul, my Apostolic Friend, according to the Divine and Exalted Will of God the Father Almighty, in order to join our efforts in the Teaching of the Good News. We already knew, despite the absence of the Bible, of theological works, of the example of the Saints of humanity, that our mission on earth was blessed by God, lifted by Christ, and illuminated by the Holy Spirit, according to the Teachings we received every day through the Gift of Paul. For Paul, who became Saint Paul the Apostle, had an intimate and unique relationship with Christ, which I will discuss in detail in this book.

Alleluia! Alleluia! Alleluia! Blessed is he who reads and studies the Epistles of Saint Paul, for Saint Paul is a True Emissary of Christ. Amen. Alleluia!

Saint Barnabas Speaks

*M*y children, listen to me well. I am here in Heaven, very close by my Friend Paul and Christ Jesus, our Savior and our God, and I am also very close to you at this time you are reading these Lines.

The transcendental operations of the Holy Spirit allow us to visit you as we wish, no matter where you are going, what you are thinking about, or what you are doing. We are independent of the state of your soul; however, your prayers and intentions regarding us are attracting us a lot more easily. Thus, dear child, never neglect to be aware that there are several Divine Beings very much near you, equally compassionate, equally loving, and equally capable of performing miracles for you.

Alleluia! Alleluia! Alleluia! Blessed is he who prays and honors the visits of the Saints in Paradise, for our Blessings upon this one so increase. Amen. Alleluia!

Saint Barnabas Speaks

My children, I am delighted to speak to you today about life in Paradise.

Here, in the Kingdom of the Father of all, the Beatitudes promised to the souls converted to Christ truly exist. The beauty of Paradise is more exquisite than you can imagine! The Ineffable Music of the Celestial Spheres nurtures us with delight. Nature also exists, but here it is pristine; gardens of magnificent flowers under our feet, streams of miraculous purity, trees and vegetations of intense and vibrant colors, and gentle hills charming with beauty, compose these ineffable landscapes of the Kingdom.

We are free to walk with joy and gladness here and there in the Kingdom and to rejoice in the bounty of the Father while praising Him and adoring Him by our constant prayers.

Alleluia! Alleluia! Alleluia! Blessed are those invited to join us here in Paradise, for all that has been promised to you will be given to you. Amen. Alleluia!

Saint Barnabas Speaks

My children, I am happy to teach you the Good News today, as I have done 2,000 years ago alongside Saint Paul the Apostle.

Saint Paul the Apostle was gifted with the Grace of Clairvoyance and Clairaudience, as granted by the Father. These Miracles of the Holy Spirit led Paul to receive the Luminous Teachings of Christ directly from Him. The Letters he wrote were dictated and guided by none other than Christ Jesus Himself. I was amazed and enchanted by this miraculous and unique relationship that Paul had with Christ Jesus. My trust in Paul was boundless, knowing that our mission was blessed by God.

Alleluia! Alleluia! Alleluia! Blessed is he who hears the Good News today and who believes in the messengers of God. Amen. Alleluia!

Saint Barnabas Speaks

8

My children, remain in the joy and gladness brought about by faith in Jesus Christ, our Lord and our God.

He alone is the Way, the Truth, and the Life. He alone has saved us from the clutches of the devil. He alone has delivered us from death and the dangers of the purifying flames. He alone is Love with the Father and the Holy Spirit.

Alleluia! Alleluia! Alleluia! Blessed is he who comes in the Name of the Lord! Amen. Alleluia!

Saint Barnabas Speaks

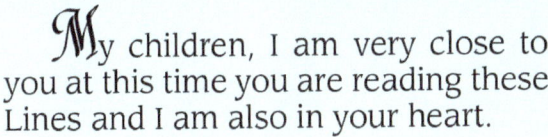

My children, I am very close to you at this time you are reading these Lines and I am also in your heart.

This ineffable phenomenon operated by the Holy Spirit enables our Energetic interactions and the accomplishment of miracles, which are destined for you according to the Mercy of God the Father. For God the Father loves you and He demonstrates it to you through reading this book (and all the other books dictated to the essence of Saint Paul on earth) and the Blessings hidden therein.

Alleluia! Alleluia! Alleluia! Blessed be this intimate moment occurring between us, a moment filled with faith and hope and raised by the Holy Spirit. Amen. Alleluia!

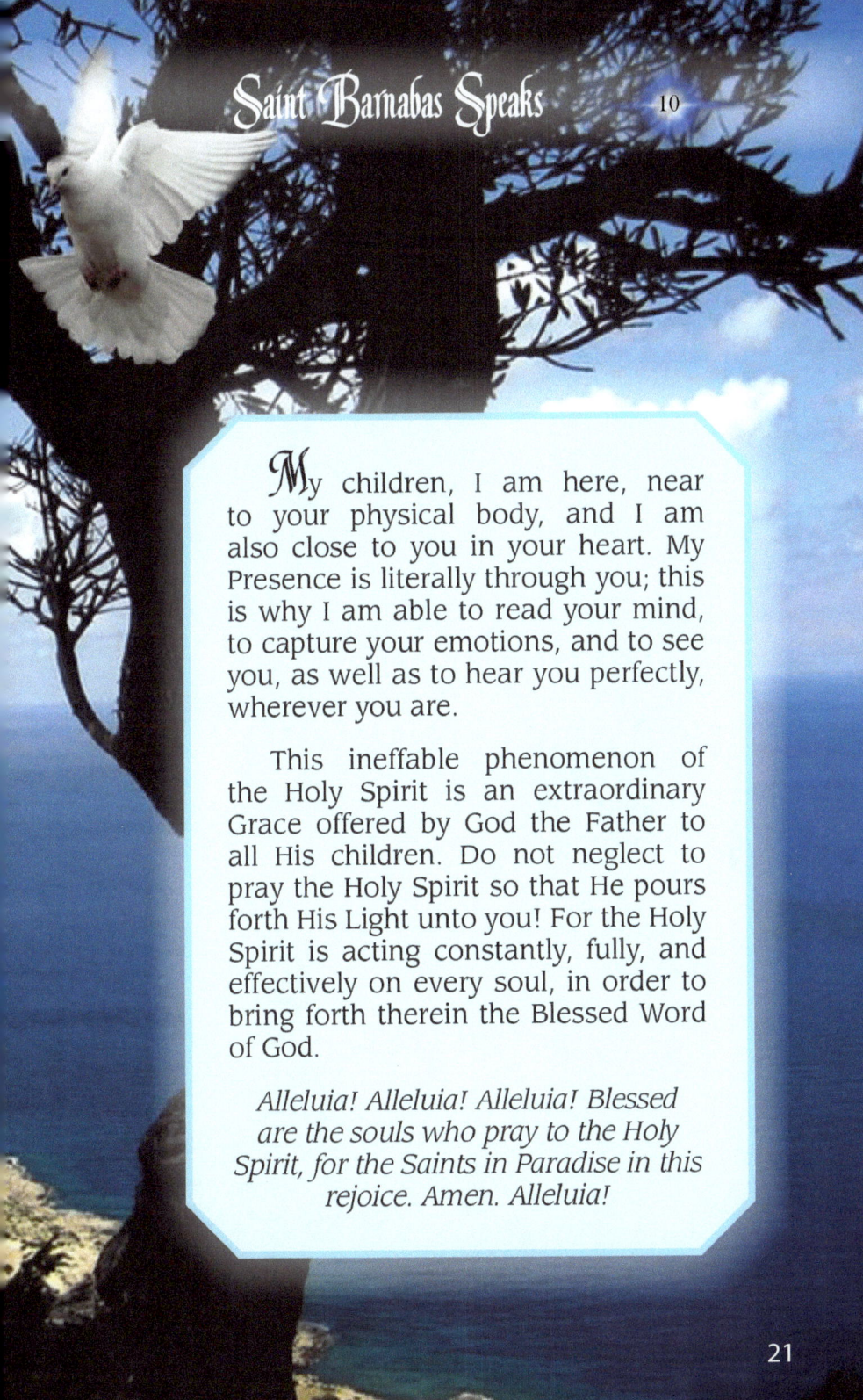

Saint Barnabas Speaks

10

My children, I am here, near to your physical body, and I am also close to you in your heart. My Presence is literally through you; this is why I am able to read your mind, to capture your emotions, and to see you, as well as to hear you perfectly, wherever you are.

This ineffable phenomenon of the Holy Spirit is an extraordinary Grace offered by God the Father to all His children. Do not neglect to pray the Holy Spirit so that He pours forth His Light unto you! For the Holy Spirit is acting constantly, fully, and effectively on every soul, in order to bring forth therein the Blessed Word of God.

Alleluia! Alleluia! Alleluia! Blessed are the souls who pray to the Holy Spirit, for the Saints in Paradise in this rejoice. Amen. Alleluia!

Alleluia! Alleluia! Alleluia! Blessed is he who is kind and charitable toward his fellowman (or a defenseless animal), for God Himself receives all these intentions and rejoices therein. Amen. Alleluia!

Saint Barnabas Speaks

My children, pay much attention to the Words written in this book of Light. My Voice, that of Saint Barnabas, a servant of God according to His Ineffable and Infinite Grace, is heard at this very moment in dictation by Marie-Josée, the essence of Saint Paul on earth. My Voice, hence transmitted to you, is destined to change your life.

I wish and pray that your soul becomes purified, rendered white as snow, before the disastrous events that lie ahead. For another war—the last one—is fast approaching. Such is the Will of God the Father Almighty.

Alleluia! Alleluia! Alleluia! Blessed is he who reads these Lines and hears my Voice, for God Himself in this rejoices. Amen. Alleluia!

Saint Barnabas Speaks

My children, be assured of my Heavenly and Cosmic help, as well as the help from Saint Paul the Apostle, the Logos of conversion to Christ Jesus.

We have prayed for you, dear reader, for a long time now, in order that you can read this book you are holding in your hands and which is blessed by God.

For the end times are drawing near and there is little time available to proceed to the complete purification of your soul.

Alleluia! Alleluia! Alleluia! Blessed is Marie-Josée, who ensures the production of this book and who is herself blessed by God. Amen. Alleluia!

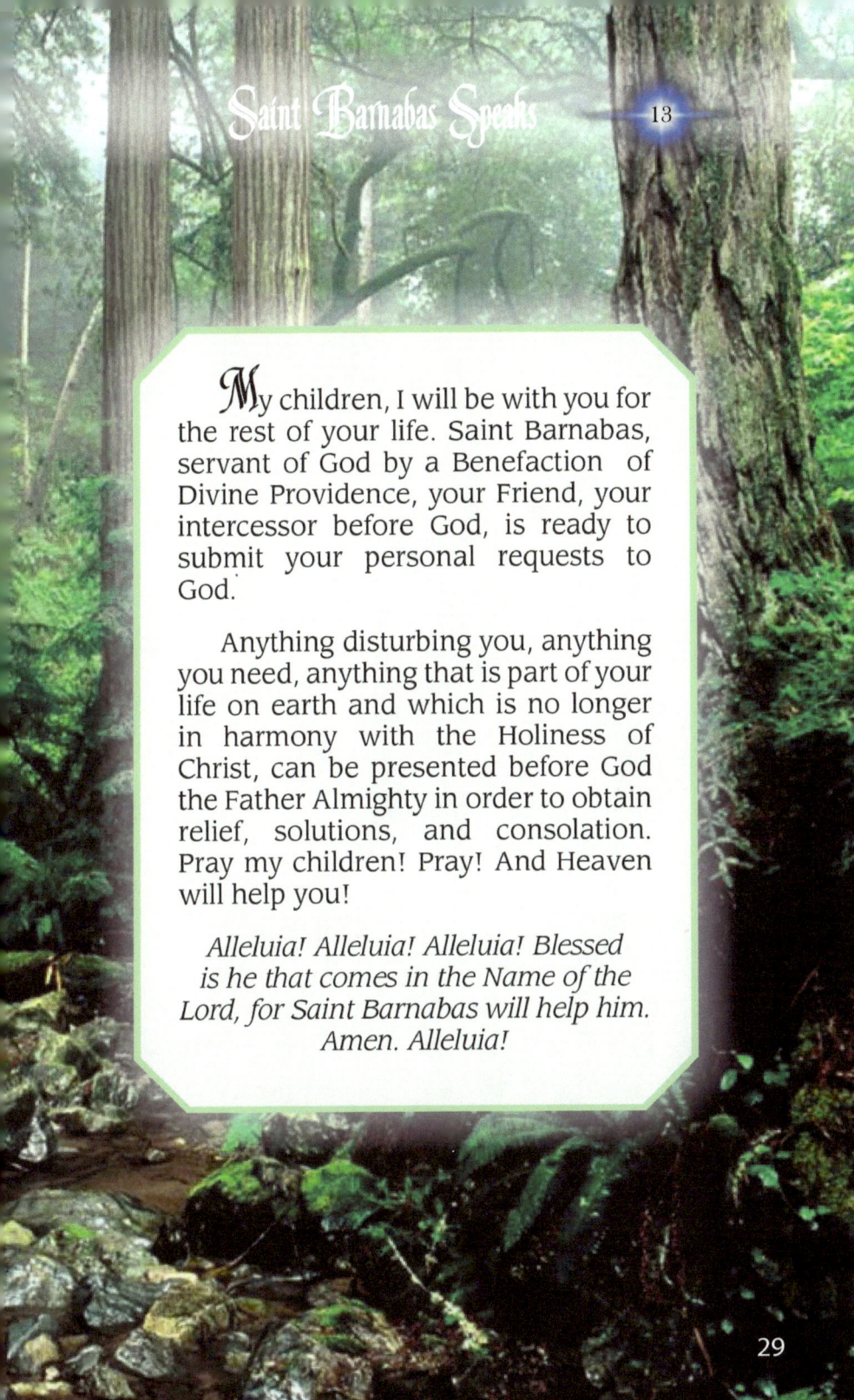

Saint Barnabas Speaks

My children, I will be with you for the rest of your life. Saint Barnabas, servant of God by a Benefaction of Divine Providence, your Friend, your intercessor before God, is ready to submit your personal requests to God.

Anything disturbing you, anything you need, anything that is part of your life on earth and which is no longer in harmony with the Holiness of Christ, can be presented before God the Father Almighty in order to obtain relief, solutions, and consolation. Pray my children! Pray! And Heaven will help you!

Alleluia! Alleluia! Alleluia! Blessed is he that comes in the Name of the Lord, for Saint Barnabas will help him. Amen. Alleluia!

Saint Barnabas Speaks

14

My children, remain much more preoccupied with the state of living nature around you and detach yourself instead from inert and illusory objects.

Christic Energy resides in everything that lives, everything that grows, and everything that dies. Just as the kingdom of animals and of plants, the mineral kingdom also contains Christic Energy. For Christic Energy, the Foundation of Life, is in itself the Spark of Divine Fire deriving from the Central Sun, and the Central Sun is at the Origin of all the Creation.

Alleluia! Alleluia! Alleluia! Blessed is he who respects all forms of life, for Christ is the Way, the Truth and the Life. Amen. Alleluia!

Saint Barnabas Speaks

My children, remain also preoccupied with the Christic state of your soul. Indeed, it is very important to be in a state of purity, holiness and harmony at the soul's level.

Proceed often to the rituals of purification by means of the Holy Sacrament of Confession. Go as often as possible to Mass and open your soul to Holiness offered by Christ the Savior through the Holy Sacrament of Eucharistic Communion. In addition, harmonize yourself with all forms of life around you: your fellowman as well as members of the kingdom of animals, plants, and minerals that come your way. For Christ is the Way, the Truth, and the Life. Amen! Alleluia!

Every tree, every insect, every fish, every bird, every grain of sand, consists in its foundation of pure Christic Substance. From this, life is formed.

Saint Barnabas Speaks

My children, I am here with you today to teach you the secrets of life among the kingdoms of the Creation.

First of all, let us speak about the animal kingdom. God the Father Almighty, our Creator, is at the Origin of all animal species inhabiting the earth. Each of them—from the smallest to the largest, those domestic and those in the wilderness, those who walk the earth, those flying in the sky, or those swimming in water—all members of the animal kingdom, thus, have been created carefully, precisely, and lovingly by God Himself. That is why God knows in detail their life cycles.

After death, God has prepared for each of them a place in a special Paradise for animals, called the "Paradise of Animals." There, they can frolic, fly, eat at satiety and relax, and be in harmony with everyone around them, without worrying about hunters, abusers, and murderers on earth. The Paradise of Animals is magnificent!

Therefore, rest assured, dear child, that every animal that you loved and who has left you, is nowhere else but in the Paradise of Animals, warmed-up, well-petted, and well-loved by God the Father Almighty.

Alleluia! Alleluia! Alleluia! Let us praise God for so much Goodness, for so much Beauty, for so much Grace, and for so much Mercy! Amen. Alleluia!

Saint Barnabas Speaks

My children, allow me to speak to you today about the plant kingdom.

Plants in general constitute all the vegetation existing in nature: trees and shrubs, flowers, ground coverings, crops planted by humans. Everything that lives and grows without being able to move by itself constitutes the plant kingdom.

The unique Spirit of a plant is called its elemental. The elemental of the plant is a living soul that is sensitive to vibrations and energies surrounding it. Indeed, the elemental is in relation with the elementals of other plants, as well as with the Holy Spirit, Christ and God the Father Almighty of the Trinity. The elemental of the plant obeys the messages and instructions received by the Higher Planes of the Creation. This is why plants are able to heal humans, if the elemental is so ordered.

Alleluia! Alleluia! Alleluia! Blessed are the elementals of plants, Sacred Vessels of Divine Will. Amen. Alleluia!

Saint Barnabas Speaks

My children, I am continuing my Teaching today regarding the plant kingdom.

Did you know that each plant has a Name in the Eyes of God? Did you know that God the Father Almighty is equally concerned with small wild flowers as the large forest of redwood trees and the reeds near streams? Did you know that God has imbued each elemental with unique virtues and powers little known to man?

It is the duty of humankind to respect, love, and discover the true nature of the elementals of nature surrounding you.

Alleluia! Alleluia! Alleluia! Blessed is he who loves nature, for in return the elementals of the same nature will love him! Amen. Alleluia!

Saint Barnabas Speaks

My children, today we continue our study of the plant kingdom.

Although plants cannot move on the earth, the elementals of the plants can actually move freely where they wish, according to the Divine Will which directs them. Consequently, the elementals can visit the sick, relieve the distressed, and repair many misdeeds by going across the ethereal dimensions of the earth. Thus, there are no restrictions of time and place when an elemental is instructed and is ordered to cure a patient remotely. The elemental joins with the Etheric Energies of the individual in need and contributes to his healing according to God's Plan.

Alleluia! Alleluia! Alleluia! Blessed are the elementals of plants, instruments of Peace participating in the Great Divine Mercy. Amen. Alleluia!

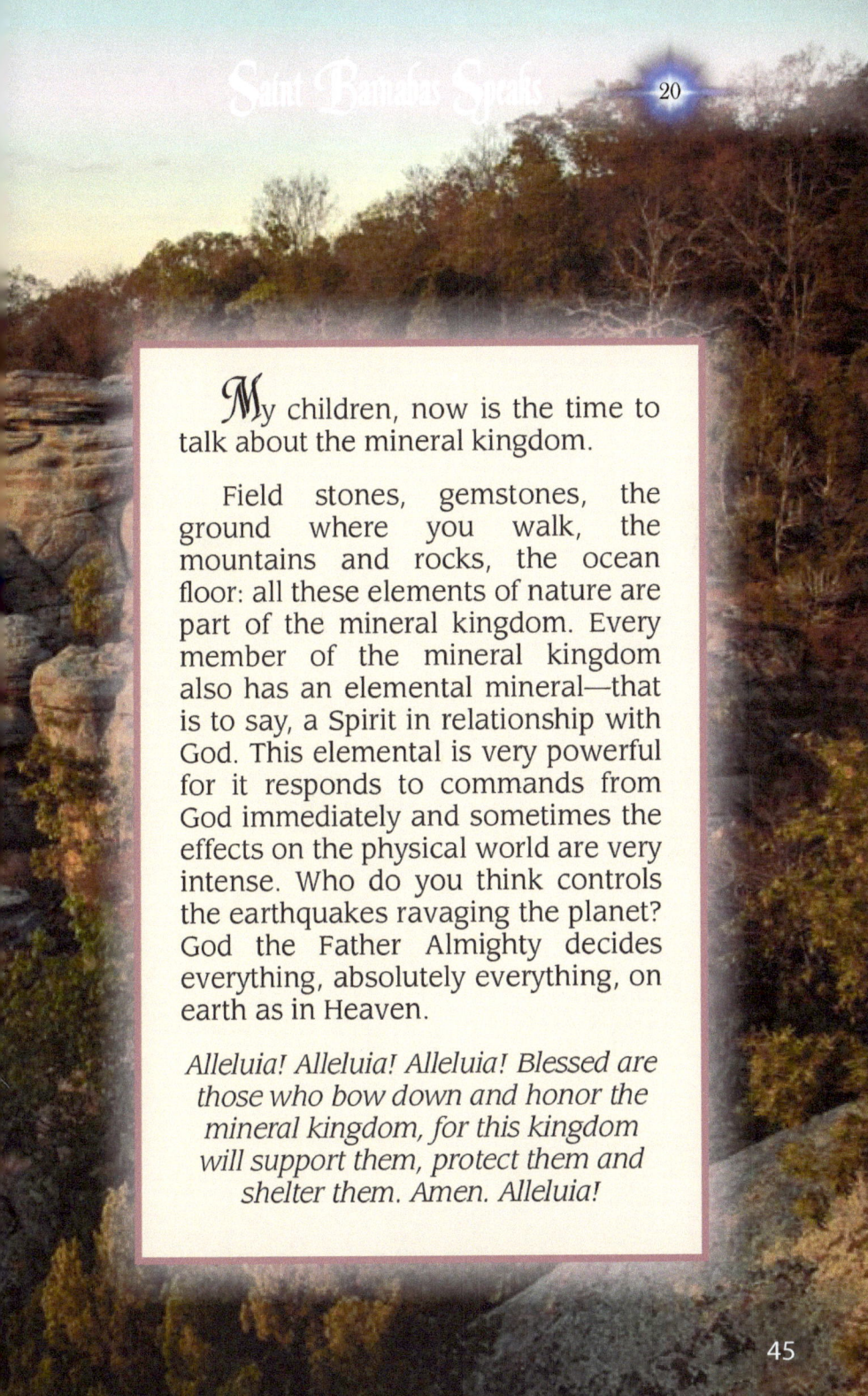

Saint Barnabas Speaks

*M*y children, now is the time to talk about the mineral kingdom.

Field stones, gemstones, the ground where you walk, the mountains and rocks, the ocean floor: all these elements of nature are part of the mineral kingdom. Every member of the mineral kingdom also has an elemental mineral—that is to say, a Spirit in relationship with God. This elemental is very powerful for it responds to commands from God immediately and sometimes the effects on the physical world are very intense. Who do you think controls the earthquakes ravaging the planet? God the Father Almighty decides everything, absolutely everything, on earth as in Heaven.

Alleluia! Alleluia! Alleluia! Blessed are those who bow down and honor the mineral kingdom, for this kingdom will support them, protect them and shelter them. Amen. Alleluia!

Field stones, gemstones, the ground where you walk, the mountains and rocks, the ocean floor: all these elements of nature are part of the mineral kingdom. Every member of the mineral kingdom also has an elemental mineral—that is to say, a spirit in relationship with God.

Saint Barnabas Speaks

21

My children, I want to discuss with you today the power of metals through their elementals.

Metals, since they cannot move or speak clearly in the eyes of men, are often ignored and ill-considered. Why are metals so important? Since their elementals are in direct relationship with God (as all the elementals of the other realms are), they contain in their physical bodies a phenomenal Energetic power unknown to men. God the Father Almighty can use this Energy at Will, through their elemental intelligence, in order to accomplish His Divine Plan.

Alleluia! Alleluia! Alleluia! Blessed are the elementals of metals and minerals, friends of God and friends of men. Amen! Alleluia!

Saint Barnabas Speaks

My children, I am here with you today, near by you, and I am discussing with you all the kingdoms that God has created.

The Kingdom of Heaven, of Ineffable Beauty, Supreme in its Powers over the entire earth, dazzling of Christic Light, is awaiting you and is offering you a glorious entry among us.

For this book blessed by God will take you directly to its Golden Gates, at the exact minute ordained and appointed by the Divine Will of God That *is*. For everything, absolutely everything on earth, is subject to His Almighty Will.

Other kingdoms conceived by God will be discussed later in this book.

Alleluia! Alleluia! Alleluia! Blessed are the readers of this book, beloved children of God, for whom He has reserved a unique place in His Kingdom. Amen! Alleluia!

Saint Barnabas Speaks

My children, I am pleased to speak to you today of earthly kingdoms, consisting of mineral, plant, and animal kingdoms.

These kingdoms, conceived by God at the beginning of the Creation, have evolved according to the Divine Will of the Father and according to His Plan of Salvation. Every little and big soul inhabiting these kingdoms is equally loved, equally protected, and equally saved by the Divine Grace that generated them, the Grace of the Father Creator. For the Father Creator loves perfectly, knows perfectly, and leads back perfectly to Him everything that comes from Him, and by that I mean everything that is contained in His Creation.

Alleluia! Alleluia ! Alleluia! Blessed be God and His Creation, the Love of God manifested and honored through all the souls of the earthly kingdoms that He created. Amen. Alleluia!

Saint Barnabas Speaks — 24

My children, live in the Glory and hope of the Kingdom promised to you, live in the Harmony and Love taught by Christ our Savior and our God, and live in peace and enchantment in the midst of the earthly kingdoms surrounding you. For the Grace of God is given to you here and today, through this book blessed by Him.

Alleluia! Alleluia! Alleluia! Blessed is he who is invited to the Father's Golden Table, on earth as in Heaven. Amen! Alleluia!

Saint Barnabas Speaks

My children, never forget the Powers of Christ contained in all living matter.

Every tree, every insect, every fish, every bird, every grain of sand, is made up in its foundation of Pure Christic Substance. From this, life is formed. That is why every spark of life existing in nature contains the Vibrations of Christ, in resonance with the Holy Divine Trinity, and subject to the Great Law and Will of the Father. For God the Father Almighty is present everywhere, at all times, and forever.

Alleluia! Alleluia! Alleluia! Blessed is he who respects life existing in all things, for God dwells therein. Amen. Alleluia!

Every little and big soul inhabiting the animal kingdom is equally loved, equally protected, and equally saved by the Divine Grace that generated them, the Grace of the Father Creator.

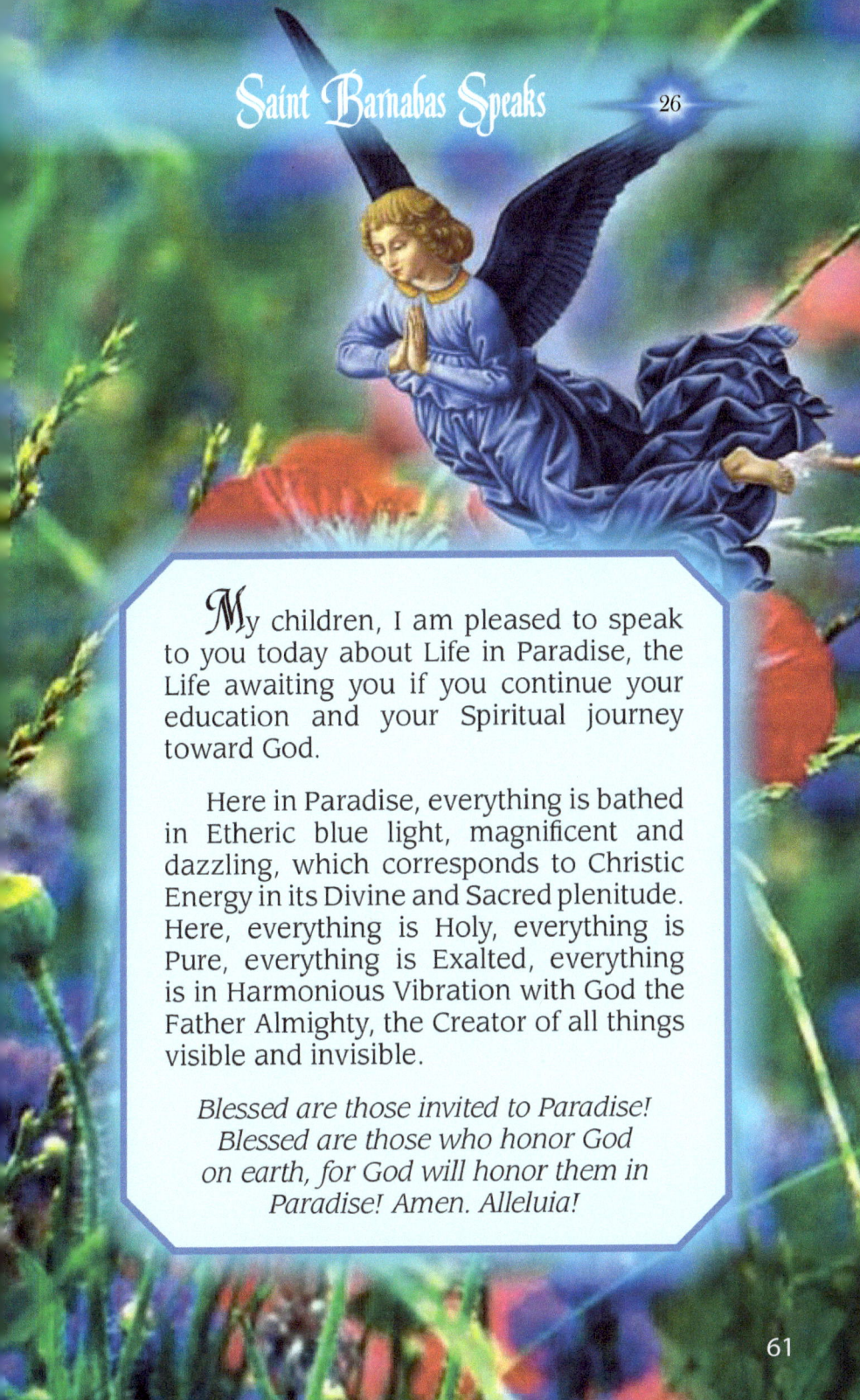

Saint Barnabas Speaks

26

My children, I am pleased to speak to you today about Life in Paradise, the Life awaiting you if you continue your education and your Spiritual journey toward God.

Here in Paradise, everything is bathed in Etheric blue light, magnificent and dazzling, which corresponds to Christic Energy in its Divine and Sacred plenitude. Here, everything is Holy, everything is Pure, everything is Exalted, everything is in Harmonious Vibration with God the Father Almighty, the Creator of all things visible and invisible.

Blessed are those invited to Paradise! Blessed are those who honor God on earth, for God will honor them in Paradise! Amen. Alleluia!

Saint Barnabas Speaks

My children, be on earth the Father's Glory and this Glory will spread around you.

Kindness and generosity, beautiful and grand virtues delighting the Father, were the Graces that the Father gave me during my life on earth.

Gentleness, patience, community service, sharing, and humility, are also virtues accompanying and ennobling the attributes of kindness and generosity.

Be assured that God the Father Almighty takes delight in each act of charity and kindness accomplished around you and in His Name. For each generous and charitable act intended for your fellowman (or a defenseless animal, or a beautiful garden under your care) is, in fact, received by God Himself. Charity toward your fellowman and charity toward God are one and the same.

Alleluia! Alleluia! Alleluia! Blessed is he who is kind and charitable toward his fellowman, for God Himself receives all these intentions and rejoices therein. Amen. Alleluia!

Saint Barnabas Speaks

My children, rejoice and be glad for the Kingdom of God is promised to you, today, through these Lines blessed by God.

I say unto you, I say unto you verily, listen and apply the Teachings of Christ that you are receiving through His messengers who have spoken to you through the Bible and other theological works during the history of humanity. Especially, because of events that are fast approaching, read and read again all the books in this collection. For they are intended for you, you dear reader, thanks to the Love and Apostolic devotion of Saint Paul the Apostle, utilizing the instrument of His essence on earth, Marie-Josée T., and allowed by God the Father Almighty. For the Father has leaned over your soul, dear child, dear heart in search of Him, and He is pouring forth His Blessings unto you today.

Alleluia! Alleluia! Alleluia! Blessed is he who reads these Lines and believes, for God Himself allowed this Blessed instant. Amen. Alleluia!

Saint Barnabas Speaks

My children, I am delighted today to speak to you about my life on earth, when I was Barnabas.

I grew up at my parents' farm north of Jerusalem. My childhood life was simple and purified by the proximity of nature and farm animals. I inherited this land at the time of my parents' death. Therefore I was able to contribute financially to our Apostolic mission through the sale of these lands.

I was raised in the Jewish religion and my parents were very pious. I heard about the Teachings of Jesus of Nazareth, a Jewish Prophet among us, and I went to several of His public gatherings. Thereafter, my life took an extraordinary turn.

Alleluia! Alleluia! Alleluia! Blessed be the Holy Land of Jerusalem, the Land that the Sacred Feet of Jesus touched. Amen. Alleluia!

Saint Barnabas Speaks

My children, I am delighted to speak to you in more detail about my life on earth.

I was a believer from the beginning of my contacts with Christ. His Teaching, His Charisma, the Miracles He accomplished on earth were extraordinary at that time—as they remain today. All, without exception, spoke of Him. We wanted to believe in the Messiah! Oh yes! We wanted to believe in Him! Oh yes!

Alleluia! Alleluia! Alleluia! Blessed be the people of Israel, people chosen by God to hear His Word first. Amen. Alleluia!

Pray! Pray! Pray!
~ Barnabas

Saint Barnabas Speaks

My children, I continue today with you my experience of life on earth at the time of Jesus of Nazareth.

Everyone was fascinated and subjugated by this new Master Who was the Son of God, the long awaited Messiah. Such joy among us, the early followers of Jesus of Nazareth! So much hope of reconciliation with God the Father Almighty! So much hope in the Kingdom of Heaven promised to us!

And I am speaking to you from here, Paradise where I live, and which is waiting for you too! Life on earth is short, my children. Be patient and vigilant, work hard in the mission given by God for you, pray constantly, confess your trespasses against God and men; and shortly, very shortly, you will be among us here in Paradise! Amen. Alleluia!

Saint Barnabas Speaks

My children, let me speak to you today about Jesus of Nazareth. Beautiful, tall, illuminated from the inside and the outside, this Human Being seemed to have been deposited directly by the Father from Heaven.

He was of absolute and perpetual calm, always smiling and affable to all, of inner Peace and Harmony imperturbable and at all times. People rushed around Him in order to touch Him, to obtain His Blessing and His Healing.

And He, always bathed in a Halo of Holiness, Wisdom, and Serenity, gave Himself completely and lovingly, without losing anything of His physical composure and of His state of evident recollection with God Himself.

Alleluia! Alleluia! Alleluia! Blessed be Jesus of Nazareth, Who is the Son of the Living God, our Savior and our God! Amen. Alleluia!

Saint Barnabas Speaks

My children, I am delighted to speak to you now of what awaits you in Paradise. I have already spoken in the past of the exquisite Beauty of Paradise. Today, I speak of our duties.

Here in Paradise, every one of us prays for the all the souls on earth, for the salvation of all of you—continuously. Saint Paul the Apostle, my Friend in the Good News, is the Director of all the prayers taking place constantly in Paradise. He ensures that everyone here in Paradise, including the Angels of God, the Saints in Paradise, and the pure Souls, pray without ceasing, according to the needs of humans and of nature, through the Glorious Name of Jesus Christ, our Savior and our King, and the Immaculate Heart of Mary.

Alleluia! Alleluia! Alleluia! Blessed are those invited to Paradise, at the Father's Golden Table, where prayer is Holy. Amen! Alleluia!

Saint Barnabas Speaks

My children, always remain in the hope of our prayers for you and of our Divine Protection. We, the Saints in Paradise, messengers of God the Father Almighty, Celestial Friends of Christ our Savior, hold in our hands all the resources and solutions required for the relief of all your troubles and complaints. Be not afraid! Pray instead!

Pray to God the Father Almighty in order to obtain His Divine Mercy, and ask for our intercessions simultaneously.

Simply say: "Saint Barnabas, intercede for me, before God the Father Almighty, for the obtention of [requested favor], by virtue of your Gift of Charity and your Gift of Kindness, through the Glorious Name of our Lord Jesus Christ and the Immaculate Heart of Mary. Amen." Alleluia!

Saint Barnabas Speaks

My children, I hasten to speak to you about my particular role in Paradise. Indeed, each of us here in Paradise is assigned specific and unique functions, decided by God the Father Almighty Himself.

For example, you now know that Saint Paul the Apostle is the Director of all the prayers taking place in Heaven for humanity on earth. Blessed is Saint Paul the Apostle and blessed is the essence of Saint Paul on earth! Amen. Alleluia!

My duties, therefore, are related to the preservation and the protection of all members of the animal kingdom, the plant kingdom, and the mineral kingdom on earth.

Yes, I have much more Power on earth than you can imagine and I give to God the Father Almighty my endless gratitude for so much Mercy on my soul. Amen! Alleluia!

My children, be on earth the Father's glory

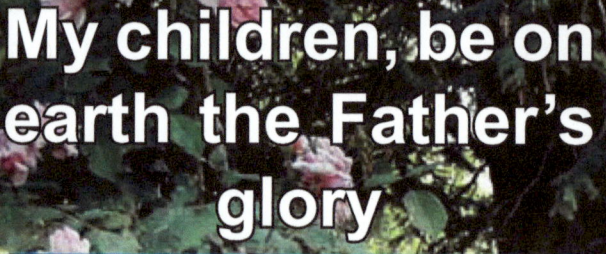

and this glory will spread around you.

Saint Barnabas Speaks

My children, let me tell you about the joys and beatitudes of living next to Jesus the Christ our Savior, as well as to the other Saints in Paradise, to the pure Souls, to the Angels of God, to the Most Blessed Virgin Mary, to the Holy Spirit, and to God the Father Almighty.

Here, there is no concept of time. Consequently, we all live in the present moment, without beginning and without end, completed and unfinished, from Holy instant to Holy instant, for ever and ever; and here, nothing ages and nothing passes. Here in Paradise, the Kingdom of God promised by Christ our Savior, the joys and beatitudes of the Great Beyond can not be expressed by intellectual concepts of languages and words. For Paradise is Ineffable in its Beauty, its Eternity, and its Supremacy over earth.

Alleluia! Alleluia! Alleluia! Blessed are those invited to the promised Paradise! Amen. Alleluia!

Saint Barnabas Speaks

My children, I teach you today about the precise transition from life to death and ultimately to Eternal Life.

The passage that is death is an illusion from your three-dimensional side; the heart stops beating, the lungs stop breathing, the body stiffens and cools. This is an event of extreme sadness for you to see, dear humans, due to its tragic and irreversible aspect. However, remember that the soul was attached to the body for a limited period of time—the time needed for a life term on earth. The soul is Eternal, as you already know, implying that it was generated at the beginning of the Creation by God and that it will never end. Consequently, your soul is in a period of exile on earth, that is to say, in a learning period of the Laws governing the Creation, as conceived by God the Father Almighty. For God the Father Almighty is the Creator of all souls who inhabit the earth and Heaven, and His Love for His Creation is Infinite.

Alleluia! Alleluia! Alleluia! Blessed be God the Father Almighty, Creator of all souls by Infinite Love. Amen. Alleluia!

My children, I want you to understand well what happens in your physical body at the time of death.

As explained earlier, death, while tragic, is necessary for the completion at the term of life in order to leave the body in three dimensions. The soul, being Eternal, returns to the Superior Planes of Creation to be examined and judged. God the Father Almighty, Who decides everything, with regards to everything, and at all times, decide the fate of the soul when it returns in the Great Beyond.

Angels of God prepare to bring the soul to Paradise in a beautiful triumphal parade if God the Father decides that the soul is pure enough to enter Paradise. Otherwise, the fallen soul of Paradise is delivered (with much sadness in the Great Beyond) into the hands of satan and of his dark angels. Purgatory, which truly exists, is a transition of purification for the impure souls. This transition is decided by God the Father, and for a period determined by God the Father, in conditions that I would rather not describe here...

Rest assured, dear child, dear soul blessed by God through this miraculous book that you are reading—a unique and precious Benediction in your life—that I, Saint Barnabas, as well as the other Saints in Paradise, love you, guide you, and protect you, so to allow your royal entrance into Paradise! Amen. Alleluia!

S†††††B

Saint Barnabas Speaks

My children, I hasten to explain in more detail the events surrounding the physical death.

When the soul is about to leave the physical body, the soul reconstitutes itself in a totality, which separates from the physical body in which it was locked. The soul, therefore, realizes quickly and suddenly the cosmic value in the Eyes of God of his life on earth that was just completed. Did he love as Christ? Did he forgive as Christ? Was he charitable as Christ? Did he hope for the Kingdom of God as Christ?

The soul already knows the answer to these questions when preparing to leave the body. This vision is either Glorious of Christic Light or it is tragic of darkness of demons.

Pray! Pray! Pray! Choose today what you will see at the minute of your death! Amen. Alleluia!

Saint Barnabas Speaks

40

My children, I want to speak to you today about the tragic cases of committed suicides.

The soul, as you know, is Eternal. It is also Sacred, in the sense that it was created by God, and thus belongs to God. God decides the term of life on earth and He chooses the body and its attributes for this life for each of us.

Committing suicide is the most serious mistake that a soul can commit against God. Not only does the soul deny the Sacredness of Life, the soul also denies God, for the soul that self-destructs his body given by God through Love has turned against God and has given himself to satan. Satan gladdens of these souls he has stolen from God. Unfortunately, this soul will suffer the fires of hell and the constant and monstrous view of satan in all its loathsome hideousness.

Pray, my children, pray to prevent souls from committing the unpardonable sin of suicide! I love you. Amen. Alleluia!

For the Holy Spirit is acting constantly, fully, and effectively on every soul, in order to bring forth therein the gentle Word of God.

Saint Barnabas Speaks

My children, I am delighted to continue my discussion of the events surrounding death.

The Angels of God, who are made of Divine Light in the service of Divine Will, have different functions in Heaven. A group of Angels, hereinafter called the Angels of Death, work alongside the dying souls on earth to facilitate the passage that is death toward a felicitous outcome, that is to say, the royal entry of this soul in the Kingdom of God.

The Angels of Death work assiduously to awaken the soul during the last moments of life and hope, and bring this soul to confession and repentance of sins committed during its existence on earth. They have been intermediaries in several miracles, which have occurred in the very last moments of any possible salvation of souls who have been redeemed just before death.

They have the Power to send a priest as well as the Sacraments necessary for the rapid and efficient purification of the soul while there is still time.

Above all, Saint Michael the Archangel, Supreme Power in Paradise, often intervenes on behalf of souls who merit His help. We shall soon speak in more detail about Saint Michael the Archangel.

Alleluia! Alleluia! Alleluia! Blessed are the souls who merit the help of the Angels of God, for God Himself in this rejoices. Amen. Alleluia!

Saint Barnabas Speaks

*M*y children, be very clear here that my purpose in these Writings is not for you to rely solely on divine help at the last resort to allow you to go to Paradise. Of course not!

You must prepare now, for you do not know the date and time of your departure from earth. Only God knows! Today may be the last day of your existence! Get ready today! And the last seconds of your life, no matter when they take place, will be peaceful and merry, surrounded by countless Angels who have arrived to celebrate and welcome you in the midst of songs of glory and gladness.

Alleluia! Alleluia! Alleluia! Blessed are the souls who are preparing their death today, for today, their passages unto death are already facilitated. Amen. Alleluia!

Saint Barnabas Speaks

My children, I am in Heaven, from where I am speaking to you today. Shortly (as life on earth is very short) you will be with me in Paradise.

Such gladness to embrace you at the time of your royal entry in the House of God! For I have followed you for a long time, I have observed you, I have loved you, I have supported you, and I have encouraged you for a lot longer than you can imagine. In addition to my Holiness, my Gift of Charity and Kindness have allowed me to draw you to me, dear little soul, who is growing in charity and in kindness every day, thanks to my Teaching joining that of Christ.

Alleluia! Alleluia! Alleluia! Blessed be the soul who is charitable and kind, for God the Father Almighty will be charitable and kind toward this soul. Amen. Alleluia!

Saint Barnabas Speaks

My children, be always vigilant of the ego and the manipulations of the devil. The devil always tries to make you topple over into error and into offense against God and men. The goal of the demon is to attract you and recruit you into his army of loathsome and dark creatures. Always be on your guard! And do not be tempted by the illusion that is the short life on earth.

Shortly, with our Divine help, everything will be clear and your Spirit will live with us in Paradise, for ever and ever. Amen. Alleluia!

Saint Barnabas Speaks

45

My children, I am pleased to speak to you about Saint Michael the Archangel.

Saint Michael the Archangel is the most elevated Angel of all the Creation. His Angelic Power on earth as in Heaven is unsurpassed among the other Angels, and cannot be properly appreciated by men. He is the Angel closest to God, and His Angelic Light reigns everywhere and envelops the whole world with incomparable Strength, Courage, and Protection.

Pray often to Saint Michael the Archangel and He will hasten to protect you and support you on your path of return toward God.

Alleluia! Alleluia! Alleluia! Blessed is he who prays to Saint Michael the Archangel, for God Himself in this rejoices. Amen. Alleluia!

Saint Barnabas Speaks

My children, let me delight in speaking to you in greater length about Saint Michael the Archangel.

Saint Michael, the most elevated Angel as already mentioned, is capable of performing countless miracles for you. His Powers are limitless from the perspective of men. He is defending you against all aspects of the devil, including the manipulation of the mind and of emotions produced by the devil in the human intellect and heart.

Saint Michael also specializes in what concern the events surrounding death. He directs the Angels of death who draw near to the dying souls, and He has the Power to put into action in an urgent manner the terrestrial and Celestial resources needed for the salvation of this soul, according to the Will of God. For Saint Michael the Archangel executes perfectly the Will of God, and He allows the perfect execution of this same Will by all Divine means and Powers available to Him on earth as in Heaven.

Alleluia! Alleluia! Alleluia! Blessed be Saint Michael the Archangel, Angel blessed by God and Angel of the salvation of men! Amen. Alleluia!

Saint Barnabas Speaks

My children, allow me today to speak with you about the future of planet earth.

The earth has generated tremendous debts toward God throughout its history, because of the imbalance that has developed between humanity and the kingdoms of animals, plants, and minerals. The situation on earth is now irreversible and must be remedied.

The terrible events drawing near aim at the regeneration of mankind according to an axis based on Christ alone, and the harmony between humanity and the kingdoms. It is sad but it is true that only a Great Global Event of Purification will be able to regenerate planet earth, according to the Will of God the Father Almighty.

*Alleluia! Alleluia! Alleluia!
Blessed be God's Great
Plan of Salvation, for a New
Day will appear on earth.
Amen. Alleluia!*

My children, my friends, this concludes my presentation. I look forward in advance of my meeting with you in Paradise. Be strong during the events just ahead.

Read and read again all the books of this collection. You will find therein the paths that will guide you to Paradise.

I bless you in the Name of the Father, and of the Son, and of the Holy Spirit.

I love you.

Saint Barnabas

Afterword

As made evident in this book, Saint Barnabas is a wholesome saint who will walk the path of holiness with you. Know that Saint Paul is close by every time Barnabas appears—they were missionaries in the past, and their mission is still ongoing!

You will never throw rubbish on the street or out the car window anymore, as Barnabas will be vexed—he will tell you to immediately ask God for forgiveness! Your heart will break once you lose a beloved pet; however, rest assured that each animal is carried directly to heaven after they pass with the help of the angels of death.

I called my recently rescued pet Barnabas—a beat-up cat I fed regularly over a six-month period as it lounged next to the grocery store before Saint Barnabas suggested I take him home. The saint's only request was that I give the cat his name. I gladly obliged!

While Saint Barnabas is a lesser-known saint, his presence among us is as transcendent and as full as Pio, Bernadette, Joan, and Therese. Invite him to your home often—he will happily and immediately appear.

Barnabas, I love you!

Marie-Josée

About The Author

Marie-Josée Thibault's life is in no way similar to yours. When she wakes, the saints of Heaven visit her, talk to her, teach her, and pray intensely with her. When such mystical sessions draw to a close, she greets with great respect and deep reverence the Masters of the Heavenly Court. This servant of the Lord spends the rest of the day in the company of her guardian angel, who continues her spiritual education and ceaselessly protects her from the perils of this fallen world.

Bestowed by the Heavenly Father, her gifts of clairvoyance and clairaudience allow her to remain in continuous contact with the supernatural dimension juxtaposed with ours, where the soul is born of the Spirit through Jesus and Mary. She prays that, one day soon, the entire human race will give glory to the Father, the Son, and the Holy Spirit.

Also By The Author

Saint Padre Pio Speaks: Book 1

Abba, Your Father, Speaks: Book I

Abba, Your Father, Speaks: Book II

Angel Gabriel Speaks: Book 1

Saint Beethoven Speaks: Book 1

Saint Bernadette Speaks Book 1

Dear Humanity: Book 1

Dear Humanity: Book 2

Saint Therese of Lisieux Speaks: Book 1

Saint Joan of Arc Speaks

Saint Martin de Porres Speaks - Book 1

FREE DOWNLOAD

Get your free copy of: "Saint Padre Pio Speaks: Book 1" when you sign up to the author's VIP mailing list! Get started here:

www.abbamyfatheriloveyou.com

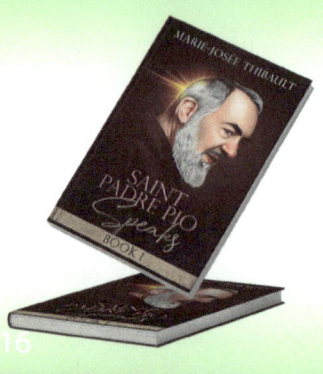